Central Virginia Heritage

Spring/Summer 2021   volume 37, number 1/2

Editor: Jean L. Cooper

A publication of the Central Virginia Genealogical Association
P.O. Box 817, Earlysville, VA 22936-0817 * website: cvga.avenue.org
© 2021 Central Virginia Genealogical Association

ISSN: 1043-4895 (print), ISSN:2472-4629 (online), ISBN: 979-8533014168 (print: v.37 no.1/2)

Try a New Approach for Genealogy Research During [the] Pandemic[1]

Augusta (GA) Genealogical Society

Many people are still limiting their excursions from home due to the COVID-19 pandemic. Even though the [Georgia] governor has approved for most commercial businesses to open, most government sources used by genealogists remain closed or have very limited hours. While "sheltering in place," this is a good time to look over your family tree and consider new approaches to your research.

One tool to consider is preparing a timeline, which can be used to organize and assess the information you have already uncovered about your ancestor. Genealogy research timelines can help to examine an ancestor's life from a historical perspective, uncover inconsistencies, highlight gaps in your research, find duplicate names, find two men with the same name, and organize the facts for each person in a specific line.

Another tool that may help with your research is a migration map of your ancestors. This will provide information on when your ancestor lived in a specific place and in some instances when they moved. The migration map will also show you where information is missing. By considering the migration pattern between the two places your ancestor lived, you may discover clues on the possible routes taken. Using these routes, look for records created during this time in this place. This is especially useful when trying to locate family records, such as census records, church information and even documents such as wills. With this information you can fill in the gaps in the timeline of a particular ancestor.

Once you have reviewed your timeline or migration map, you can determine what needs to be researched. Now it's time to consider your Research Plan and whether the plan you are using is still an effective tool. Review your goals and make a new Research Plan if the old one is not meeting your present needs.

Although a research plan cannot guarantee results, it does guarantee thoroughness and efficiency, which are the best uses of the available

---

[1] Augusta (GA) Genealogical Society. "Genealogy Column: Try a new approach for genealogy research during pandemic." *Augusta Chronicle*, July 19, 2020. https://www.augustachronicle.com/story/news/coronavirus/2020/07/19/genealogy-column-try-new-approach-for-genealogy-research-during-pandemic/114774968/

resources and time. A research plan ensures that no stone is left unturned.

With your plan in mind, now it is time to start digging to find those records. Spending time researching in the archives and in the collections, the genealogist can discover what records still exist and what information is contained therein.

Since most archives and libraries are still closed at this time, a good way to continue your research is by using the computer. Because of the pandemic, many government archives have placed additional files online, which benefit the genealogist. Others have placed indexes on their websites that will provide source and availability information for use when you can visit these institutions.

Let your fingers do the walking for now. Some sources are governmental like Archives.gov, National Archives and Records Administration (NARA), state archives and historical societies. Additionally, there are many county and university libraries, such as Allen County Public Library, Digital Public Library of America, Harvard Open Collections Program, and HathiTrust.

There are a number of other sources available on the Internet, many of them free. Some are dedicated to genealogy only, while others are historical newspapers and international websites.

There are many paid subscription sites as well that have genealogical information, software, and historical information available. If you are not interested in paid subscription services, from time to time, some will open their files for specific periods, such as to commemorate holidays like Independence Day or the end of a World War. Check these sites often because they do not usually advertise these specials except on their sites.

Many families are mentioned in books where the copyright has expired. These sources will allow you to download a copy for later review. There are other books on the Internet where only a few pages can be downloaded at a time.

"Sheltering in place" can be an excellent time to search for new resources to use to fill in some of those empty spaces on the family tree. Happy Hunting.

If you have questions, email with "Ancestor Search" in the subject line to AugustaGenSociety @comcast.net.

Reprinted courtesy of the Augusta (GA) Genealogical Society and the Augusta Chronicle, *Augusta, Georgia. Used with permission.*

Genealogy Tip of the Day

Original Versus Derivative[2]

Sources are said to be original or derivative.

The original source is, generally speaking, the original document in its original form. My birth certificate, on file in the county office in the county where I was born is my original birth certificate. The little card my parents were given with my date and place of birth and certificate number-that is derivative because it was created from the original. The photocopy of the certificate that I had made years ago–that's derivative because it is a copy of the original certificate. That "certification of live birth" I got a few years back because I needed it (and that is a typed transcription of my name, date and place of birth, and names and places of birth for my parents) is also a derivative copy–because it was created from information obtained from the original. These copies are all official legal documents and have the raised seal.

But they are derivative because the original was used as the source of the information–either via a transcription or a photocopy.

Calling them derivative does not mean that they are invalid or fraudulent. It just means they are not the original birth certificate on file in the court house.

---

[2] Genealogy Tip of the Day, 4 January 2021. Reprinted courtesy of Michael John Neill, genealogytipoftheday.com

John Burnley vs. William Crenshaw, Louisa County, VA, 1801[3]

Transcribed by Jean L. Cooper

This 11-page chancery folder is small, but mighty! It is rich with information about the Crenshaw and Burnley families. These two surnames have many representatives in Central Virginia. *[N.B. In this transcription, I have modernized punctuation in order to make it easier for the reader. — The Editor]*

Bill of Complaint

To the worshipfull the Justices of Louisa County Court sitting in Chancery. Humbly complaining shewith to the Court that your Orators and Oratrixes, Jno. Burnley & Susannah his wife, formerly Susannah Crenshaw; William Dickerson and Sarah his wife, formerly Sarah Crenshaw; David Crenshaw; Chs. Crenshaw; Jno. Crenshaw and his wife Mary formerly Mary Crenshaw; Joel Crenshaw; William Fretwell and Jimmima his wife formerly Jimmima Crenshaw; Thos. Fretwell and Agness his wife formerly Agness Crenshaw; Joel Crenshaw, son of Thos. Crenshaw & Ann his wife, now decd. who was formerly Ann Crenshaw; [illegible] Davis & Frances his wife formerly Frances Crenshaw, daughter of Thos. Crenshaw & wife, which with Chapman Crenshaw and Freeborn Crenshaw infant children of sd. Thos. Crenshaw that your Orators & Oratrixes are the children and legal [legatees?] of William Crenshaw decd. late of this county, to wit: Susannah Burnley, Sarah Dickerson, David Crenshaw, Chs. Crenshaw, Thos. Crenshaw, [Jno?] Crenshaw, Agness Fretwell, Jimmima Fretwell, Mary Crenshaw, and that Joel Crenshaw, Francis Davis, Chapman Crenshaw, and Freeborn Crenshaw all children of

---

[3] Louisa County (Va.) Chancery Causes, 1753-1913. *John Burnley & Susanna his wife, etc. v. Administrator of William Crenshaw etc. 1801-003.* Local Government Records Collection, Louisa County Court Records. The Library of Virginia, Richmond, Virginia. https://www.lva.virginia.gov/chancery/case_detail.asp?CFN =109-1801-003

Ann Crenshaw now decd. who intermarried with Thos. Crenshaw.

Your Orators & Oratrixes shew that Will: Crenshaw departed this life some time in the year of 1799 intestate having a considerable estate which was divided among his legal representatives, to wit, his wife & children, that the wife of sd. William had her dower in the slaves of her husband, who since the division has [illegible] departed this life whereby the slaves which were allotted to her as her dower slaves, have become the property of ye Orators & Oratrixes his children & their representatives, that they have been desireous to have the said slaves divided and for that purpose have called on William Cook who has been appointed by this worshipfull Court admr [administrator] of all the goods & chattel of the said Wm. Crenshaw decd.

But the said William [Cook] has refused to divide the same, stating that Chapman Crenshaw & Freeborn Crenshaw the children of _____ Crenshaw decd. one of the daughters of sd. William Crenshaw decd. are infants and that any amt. they may give him would not be oblygatory nor could they give them a bond to refund in case debts should come against the estate of Wm. Crenshaw.

Your Orators & Oratrixes therefore. Pray that the sd. Wm. Cook & Chapman Crenshaw & Freeborn Chrenshaw infants be made defs. to this bill & that they [?] and made to the premises… *[The manuscript copy stops here. — The Editor]*

Division of the Dower Negroes Belonging to the Estate of William Crenshaw decd.

In conformance to the decree annexed, We the Subscribers hath Divided the dower of Negroes belonging to the Estate of William Crenshaw decd. in the following Manner.

No. 1 Elijah to William Fretwell Pays £100
No. 2 Sam to John Crenshaw Pays £85
No. 3 Matt to Charles Crenshaw Pays £100
No. 4 Nancy to William Dickinson Pays £80

No. 5 Betty to Thomas Fretwell Receives £65
No. 6 Fanny & child to David Crenshaw Pays £80
No. 7 Phillis to Joel Crenshaw Receives £80
No. 8 Patty and [?hamer] to Thos. Crenshaw Receives £40
No. 9 [Jas?] bonds to John Burnley £66.2.2
Being the proportion of each Legatee

Given under Our Hands this 15th day of January 1801.

Thos. Gardiner
Matthew Grubbs
Overton Harris

1918 Pandemic

by Susan DuBar

Today's pandemic has frequently been compared to the 1918 flu epidemic. I had a cousin who died in the epidemic at the age of six. I knew about her through photographs and frequent references to her in her mother's and aunt's conversations. She and my father were double first cousins and were constant playmates but I never thought to ask my father how her death affected him.

Also in my family was a maternal cousin, Earl, who was a small-town pharmacist during the 1918 epidemic. I learned only recently about him when I found a newspaper article (one of those "human interest" stories) my grandmother had preserved. It was interesting to learn how few medicines were available then.

Earl graduated from Valparaiso University in 1908 with degrees in pharmacy and science—at the time pharmacy was a two-year course. He opened his drugstore in a small Indiana town in 1912. He stated to the reporter that before 1929 there wasn't much available to treat illness, the most popular remedies being sodium bicarbonate and aspirin. "People either died or got well—they didn't depend on much but fate." Sulfa drugs, introduced in 1929, followed later by penicillin brought about big change.

During the big flu epidemic, Earl frequently worked 16- to 18-hour days. The local doctor had about 4,000 sick people to care for, but must have done something right—he lost only two. The common flu remedy at the time was Dover's Powder, a preparation of ipecac and opium. He still had a bottle of Dover's Powder in 1965 that he kept for historic interest rather than use.

The current consensus seems to be that the most effective treatment for the 1918 flu was fresh air and bed rest.

Renew Your CVGA Membership for 2021

All memberships start January 1 of each year. You can renew and pay your dues online via PayPal. Check the CVGA website:

cvga.avenue.org

Membership with electronic newsletter: $15.00.
Membership with print newsletter: $30.00.

I shook the branches of my family tree
And took a chance to see what I might see.
I found a bootlegger, a pirate, a thief.
All ancestors of mine. Oh my! Good grief!
I found a lot more than I thought I would.
But there they are—my kin for ill or good.
—Anonymous

Peter Jefferson's Snowdon: A History of Settlement at the Horseshoe Bend
by Joanne L. Yeck
(Published as Occasional Paper number 1, of the Central Virginia Genealogical Association)
Shortwood Press, 2020.
ISBN: 979-8635444450. $15
https://www.amazon.com/Peter-Jeffersons-Snowdon-publications-Genealogical/dp/B088B833B7

Today, the modern counties of Albemarle, Buckingham, and Fluvanna converge at the Horseshoe Bend, at the village of Scottsville. This volume tells the story of settlement on the south side of the James River and the development of the plantation Peter Jefferson would call Snowdon.

Marriage Announcements in the *Daily Progress* (Charlottesville, VA) May-July 1895
transcribed by Diane Inman

[Note: The initial date on these entries is the date the announcement appeared in the newspaper, not the date of the event. These marriage notices were transcribed from the digital edition of the Charlottesville Daily Progress, digitized by The University of Virginia Library and the Jefferson Madison Regional Library from the microfilm of this newspaper. The microfilm is missing some issues of the newspaper in the early years. – Editor.]

03 May 1895 – SINCLAIR-MCNUTT – Marriage of This Young Couple in West Virginia. [Reprinted from the *Princeton (W. Va) Journal and Exponent*] – At the residence of **Mrs. E. E. McNutt**, on Tuesday, April 16, 1895, **Mr. George Burnley Sinclair** and **Miss Juanita McNutt** were united in marriage. **Rev. Eugene Blake** performed the ceremony in a very solemn and impressive manner. The Wedding March was beautifully rendered by Mrs. Blake. The groom, faultlessly attired, approached the altar with Judge McGrath, and the bride was given away by her brother, **C. R. McNutt, Esq**. The bride's costume was of white satin made *en train*, trimmed with white chiffon and duchess lace, bouquet of bride's roses. The marriage took place at 12, and dinner was announced immediately after congratulations had been offered.

At 1:30 the happy couple left for New York and other Eastern cities. They will spend a few days at the old home of the groom at Charlottesville, Va., and return to Princeton about the first of May.

The bride is the youngest daughter of the late **Dr. Robert B. McNutt**. Young, beautiful and intelligent, with many virtues and few faults, she is a universal favorite. We congratulate Mr. Sinclair most heartily.

The groom has been a resident of Princeton for some years and has made many friends since he came here. He is a trusted official of the Princeton Banking Company.

03 May 1895 — A marriage license was issued today by the clerk of the County court to **Thomas Tomlin** and **Daisy Lanum**. The marriage will take place Sunday (May 5) near Bethel church.

07 May 1895 — The marriage of **Miss Daisy Lanum** to **Mr. Thomas Tomlin** both of this county took place on the 5th Instant at Bethany Baptist Church. The Rev. John T. Randolph performed the ceremony.

08 May 1895 — Marriage of **Justice Brown**. — The marriage of **Mrs. Olene Crow** of Wolftown, Va., to **Mr. W. G. Brown** of this place, took place today at the residence of the bride.

Mrs. Crow, we are informed, is one of Madison's most highly respected and popular ladies, and a hearty welcome will be extended her on her arrival in Charlottesville.

Mr. Brown is successfully engaged in the mercantile business, and is interested in various other lucrative enterprises, and is also justice of the peace for Albemarle county.

09 May 1895 — Licensed to marry by the clerk of the County court: **John R. Sprouse** and **Rosa Gibson**.

21 May 1895 — A marriage license was issued today by the clerk of the County court to **William P. Payne** and **Rosella Thurston**.

27 May 1895 — **Mr. and Mrs. Albert L. Stephens** have issued invitations to the marriage of their daughter, **Sue Elizabeth**, to **Mr. L. (Louis) Arthur Taylor**. The ceremony will take place Thursday, June 6th at the home of the bride's parents. (in Washington, D.C.) The groom is a resident of this county, a son of the **late Judge Taylor** and is well-known in Charlottesville where for years he and his parents resided.

03 Jun 1895 — Marriages licenses were issued today by the clerk of the County court to **Dr. C. W. Kent** and **Mrs. Eleanor Miles**; **G. McCrery** and **T[illegible] Sneed**.

04 Jun 1895 — **Mr. F. D. Power** of the Garfield Memorial church, Washington, D.C., who was called here to assist in the marriage ceremony of **Dr. C. W. Kent** and **Mrs. Eleanor Miles**, returned this afternoon to his home.

KENT–MILES — Pretty June Wedding This Morning at the University of Virginia — The chapel at the University of Virginia was, this morning, the scene of the marriage of **Mrs. Eleanor Miles**, daughter of **Prof. Francis H. Smith** of the University of Virginia, to **Dr. Charles W. Kent**, professor of English Literature in that institution.

The bride entered the chapel leaning on the arm of her father, followed by the ushers and attendants. The groom with his best man, the **Hon. Henry T. Kent**, of St. Louis, awaited the bride at the chancel. The impressive service was beautifully rendered by **Dr. F. D. Power**, of the Garfield Memorial church Washington, formerly pastor of the Christian church at this city. The attendants were **Mr. Robert L. Harrison** of New York, **Dr. William Harrison** of Roanoke, **Dr. Hunter Pendleton** of the Virginia Military Institute and **Mr. Robert M. Kent, Jr.** of Roanoke. The ushers were **Mr. James H. Corbitt, Mr. Raleigh C. Minor, Mr. E. A. Craighill, Jr., Mr. Pierce Bruno, Mr. J. Duncan Smith**.

Of Dr. Kent's relations, there were present: **Mr. R. M. Kent**, of Louisa, father of the groom, **Dr. and Mrs. Woolfolk** and **Miss Kent of Louisa**, **Judge Wm. S. Gooch**, of Roanoke, **Mrs. M. L. Lane**, of Louisa.

The decoration of the chapel was beautiful, ferns and roses being used with excellent taste. After a delightful collation at the home of the bride's parents, **Dr. and Mrs. Kent** left for the West on a bridal tour followed by the good wishes of a host of friends.

07 Jun 1895 — Marriage licenses were issued yesterday in Washington, D.C. to **Mr. John D. Hartman** and **Miss Musie Reynolds; Louis A. Taylor** of Albemarle County and **Sue E Stephens**.

Married in Washington — The marriage of **Miss Musie Reynolds** to **Mr. J. D. (John Daniel) Hartman** took place yesterday in Washington, DC. The young couple are residents of Charlottesville, where they are well known and popular with their friends. The groom is connected with [illegible] and

law of Mr. H. Balz. After an absence of several days, **Mr. and Mrs. Hartman** will return to Charlottesville where they will reside. [*NOTE: This couple can be found on Findagrave.com, memorials #95439609 and #55364509.*]

Mr. and Mrs. Edward Shacklett have announced the marriage of their daughter, **Edith May**, to **Mr. J. Ashby LeHew** which is to occur Jun 29th at Cool Springs Methodist church, Delaplane, Va.

10 Jun 1895 — Invitations have been received for the marriage of **Dr. Harry T. Quackenbos** to **Miss Winterton**, both of New York city. Dr. Quackenbos was a student here several years ago.

11 Jun 1895 — Marriage of **Rev. R. E. Neighbour Dr. and Mrs. Charles Henry Planck** issued invitations to the marriage of their daughter, **Nellie Gertrude Planck** to the **Rev. Robert E. Neighbour**. The ceremony is [illegible] First Baptist church, Parsons, Kan. Mr. Neighbour is well known in Charlottesville [illegible] he conducted a successful revival. Recently he returned from Brazil, where he is a missionary of the Southern Baptist Convention. [*NOTE: This couple can be found on Findagrave.com, memorials #63943447 and #62436038.*]

Michie–Hewson — At six o'clock yesterday at the home of the bride's mother, in Philadelphia, **Miss Emily Hewson**, daughter of the late **Adindell Hewson MD** was married to **Mr. Thomas Johnson Michie**, of Baltimore, eldest son of the late **H.H. Michie** of Charlottesville. The bride was given away by her brother, **Dr. Adinell Hewson**; the groom's brother, **Mr. Geo. R.H. Michie**, of the

Charlottesville Chronicle, acting as best man. **The Rev. Alfred G. Mortimer**, D.D., of St. Mark's church performed the ceremony. *[NOTE: This couple can be found on Findagrave.com, memorials #130411310 and #130411354.]*

18 Jun 1895 — Marriage Tomorrow — **Captain T. S. Keller**, wife, and little daughter, **Mary Louise**, accompanied by **Lieutenant W. J. Keller**, left this afternoon for Orange where, tomorrow, at high noon, they will witness the marriage of **Miss Reta French Patton** to **Mr. George Gilmer** of Lynchburg. The prospective bride is well known in Charlottesville where she has been a frequent visitor. Lieutenant Keller will be one of the attendants at the marriage.

They Are Now Happy! — The marriage of **Miss L. E. Johnson** to **Mr. W. A. Powell** despite opposition from relatives of the bride, took place at 9:30 o'clock this morning at the residence of **Mr. [illegible] M. Dameron** in Fifeville, the **Rev. William K. Gwatkin** performing the ceremony. The happy groom, many years the senior of his bride, who is only seventeen, is from Rockfish, where he is engaged in merchandising. She had been visiting friends here for a week or more, where yesterday afternoon she was joined by her intended husband. The happy couple left soon after the ceremony on a northern tour.

A launch party was given at Petersburg in honor of **Dr. J. Elliott Gilpin**, of Baltimore, and **Miss Catharine T. Pleasants**, of the former city, who are to be married tomorrow.

Marriage licenses were issued yesterday by the clerk of the County court to **Charles W.**
Head and **Lillie A. Smith**; **James C. Wood** and **Maude Brubeck**; **John E. Collins** and **Myrtle A. Harlow**.

19 Jun 1895 — Collins–Harlow — Yesterday afternoon **Miss Myrtle A. Harlow**, of this city, daughter of **Mr. James Harlow** and **Mr. G. Z. Collins** were united in marriage at the Methodist parsonage by **Dr. A. C. Bledsoe**. They were accompanied by **Mr. Roscoe Amos** and his sister, **Miss Bertie**. Immediately after the marriage they departed for Scottsville, their home. The bride is an attractive young lady, and the groom is a prosperous young farmer living near Scottsville.

Marriage This Evening — The marriage of **Miss Josephine Watts**, daughter of **Mr. M. S. Watts**, to **Dr. G. Woodford Brown** will take place at 8 o'clock this evening at Mt. Moriah church, near Whitehall, this county.

Dr. J.J. Colvin, **Mr. J. F. H. Somers**, **Sheriff Lucian Watts** and family left this afternoon to witness the marriage. The bride is a niece of Sheriff Watts.

Another Happy Couple — The marriage of **Miss Florence W. Rasche** of this city, to **Mr. Gailiard P. Tucker** of Washington, D. C., took place at half-past 3 o'clock this afternoon at the residence of **Mr. George N. Bragg**, 102 Fifth street northeast. Mr. and Mrs. Tucker left on the 4:15 train for Washington, where they will reside. The **Rev. W. A. Roushe** of the Christian church performed the ceremony.

20 Jun 1895 — A license was issued in the County court today for the marriage of **Berkely Bullock**, a well-known and respected

colored man of this city, and **Harriet Fleming**. The marriage takes place Saturday.

MARRIAGE—**Miss Lillie H. Sinclair** and **Mr. C. A. Head** Are United This Morning—This morning at 11 o'clock, at the residence of **Mr. F. P. Farish**, on Hinton avenue, Belmont, **Miss Lillie B. Sinclair** was married to **Mr. Claude A. Head**—the **Rev. W. E. Gwatkin** performing the ceremony.

The company was composed almost exclusively of the immediate relatives of the young lady. She was the recipient of a large number of valuable and useful presents—tokens of appreciation from many friends. The bride, who is a stately brunette, is the daughter of **Mr. John C. Sinclair** of this county. She is very popular and has many admirers in this city. The groom is an employee of the Roanoke Machine Works, being engaged in the general store keeper's office, and is much esteemed in that community.

The happy couple departed for their future home at Roanoke on the 12:15 train on the Southern Railway.

Patton-Gilmer—A brilliant marriage took place at Orange yesterday at 12:30 o'clock at St. Thomas Episcopal church. **Miss Rita Patton** was married to **Mr. George H. Gilmer**, of Lynchburg, Va.

The best man was **Dr. Blackford**, of Lynchburg, and **Miss N. O. Grymes** was maid of honor. The ushers were **Dr. Ricketts** and **Messrs. Willie Keller** of Charlottesville, **Charles S. Houseworth**, and **Carroll Slaughter**.

The bride was given away by **Captain Keller**, of Charlottesville. **Colonel Patton and wife**, of Albemarle county, relatives of the bride, **Mrs. Craddock**, Lynchburg, sister of the groom, and the **Misses Slaughter** and **Thompson** of Culpeper were in attendance.

Pretty Home Wedding in Greene—The marriage of **Miss Beulah Carpenter** to **Mr. Thomas Jennings** took place last evening at the residence of the bride's parents, near Ruckersville, Greene county, the **Rev. William E. Gwatkin** of this place officiating. Only the relatives and a few of the intimate friends of the family were present.

The bride is a niece of **Mrs. W. T. Jones** of this city. The groom is the son of **Dr. George B. Jennings** of Greene county, and nephew of **Mr. J. W. Marshall** of this city. Mr. Mat[illegible] present at the ceremony.

22 Jun 1895—WEDDING AT WHITEHALL—**Miss Josephine Watts** and **Dr. G. W. Brown** United in Marriage—One of the most pleasant affairs that has occurred for some time was the wedding of **Dr. G. Woolford Brown** and **Miss Josephine Watts**, at Mt. Moriah church, at Whitehall, in this county.

At half-past nine o'clock on Wednesday evening, the 19th instant, the bridal party, which consisted of six maids and six gentlemen, besides the maids of honor and best man, drove from the home of the bride to the church. As the strains of the wedding march, played by **Miss Rita Rodes**, filled the church, the party entered. The ribbon girls, **Miss Ida Watts** of Stony Point, and **Miss Hattie Watts**, sister of the bride, came in first and untied ribbons for the others to enter. The maids entered, two together, and the gentleman likewise, and crossing in front of the altar took their stand on opposite sides. The flower-girls, **Misses Pauline Watts** and **Janie Ralley**, preceded the bride who, leaning on the arm of her uncle, **Mr. L. C. Watts**, advanced to meet the groom and best man in front of the altar under a large bell of flowers, where the bride's father, the **Rev. M. S. Watts**, united them in the holy bonds of matrimony.

After the ceremony the party returned to the bride's home and refreshments were served. At eleven o'clock the happy couple, accompanied by a number of friends and relatives, drove to Charlottesville and took the early morning train north.

The church was beautifully decorated with flowers and evergreens.

The attendants were **Misses Maude and Evelyn Garth, Bessie Watts, Lucy Jones, Lynn Rodes** and **Lillian Watts** of Charlestown, W. Va., and **Messrs. W. E. Coons, T. G. Garth, J.F.H. Sommers, J. W. Eure, C. K. Watts**, and **W. E. Jordan**. The maid of honor was the bride's sister, **Miss Eugenia Watts**, and **Dr. J. W. Colvin** was best man.

The bride received quite a number of handsome presents from her many friends and relatives, all of whom unite in wishing the couple a long, prosperous life of wedded bliss.

24 Jun 1895—Invitations have been received to the marriage of **Miss Regina Loeb** to **Mr. Philip H. Weil**, which is to take place Wednesday, June 26th, at 8 p.m., at Harmonie Hall, New Haven, Conn. The groom-elect is the son of **Mr. A. Weil**, a former merchant of this city. *[NOTE: In the account of the wedding on Newspapers.com in* The Morning Journal-Courier, *New Haven, CT on 27 Jun 1895, page 5, the bride's name is given as "Lena."]*

The marriage of **Miss Edith May Shacklett** to **Mr. J. A. Lahew** of this city, will take place next Wednesday afternoon at Delaplane, Fauquier county. **Mrs. C. H. Smithers** left Saturday for Delaplane, and will be a guest at the ceremony. Mr. Lahew is train dispatcher of the Southern railway.

25 Jun 1895—Head–Smith—Married at 5 o'clock p.m., Wednesday the 19th instant, at the residence of the bride's father, **Mr. William P. Smith**, near Earlysville, Albemarle county, **Miss Lillie A. Smith** to **Mr. C. W. Head**. The bride, who is a charming brunette, was attired in white silk trimmed with ribbon. She, with her four bridesmaids, carried lovely bouquets of lilies.

Immediately after the ceremony, which was performed by the **Rev. George Cook**, the newly-wedded couple, with their attendants, repaired to the home of the groom, where a reception was tendered them. The bridal presents were numerous and useful, which attested the esteem in which the young couple is held.

26 Jun 1895—WEDDING AT RED HILLS—A simple, yet beautiful, ceremony in Old Fluvanna.—**Mr. Walter E. Jervey**, of Atlanta, Ga., and **Miss Margaret H. Cocke**, of Fluvanna county, were married on Tuesday, the 18th, at "Red Hills," the hospitable home of the bride's uncle—**Dr. Dudley R. Boston**.

Rev. Valentine Jones performed the ceremony.

The wedding was a simple, yet beautiful one. The house was prettily decorated with Marguerites, and the ceremony was especially impressive. Only the immediate families and a few intimate friends were present. **Lieutenant James Jervey**, of the Engineer Corps of the army, a brother of the groom, and **Miss Waller Cocke**, youngest sister of the bride, were the attendants.

Mr. Jervey is a prominent young business man of Atlanta, where he has resided several years and made a host of friends. He is a son of **Dr. Henry Jervey** of Powhatan county, Va. His bride is the attractive and accomplished daughter of the late **Judge William Ronald Cocke**, of Fluvanna county. She is a lady of decided literary talent.

A Quiet Home Wedding — At the home of **Mr. G.W. Spooner** of Bridge street [illegible] his daughter, **Miss Daisy**, was united in marriage to **Mr. James E. Thomas, Jr.** of San Antonio, Texas, the **Rev. G. H. Spooner** of Amhurst, brother of the bride, officiating.

Mr. Thomas has been taking a course at the University this session, and is a son of **Mr. J. E. Thomas** of San Antonio, and a brother of the artist, **Seymour Thomas**, now in Paris, France.

The newly married couple left on the 2:20 train for Blue Ridge Springs, where they will spend a few weeks, and then return by way of Charlottesville to their Southern home.

Married June 25th by the **Rev. John T. Randolph**, **Mr. Reuben Sprouse** and **Miss Martha I. Marsh**, both of Albemarle.

A marriage license was issued today by the clerk of the County court to **Benjamin Gibson** and **Sallie Ann Young**. A few minutes after securing the coveted document, the couple drove to the Presbyterian manse where they were married by **Dr. G. L. Petrie**.

27 Jun 1895 — EPIDEMIC IN GREENE — But it is the Matrimonial Fever — RUCKERSVILLE, Va., June 26th — An epidemic is prevailing in this section, extraordinary in extent and character. All who are not exempt by reason of a previous attack are liable to the all pervading microbes. What is still more remarkable is that a disease known as a cold weather malady, should assume such proportions during the heated term. It is known as the "matrimonial fever."

The beautiful residence of "Mill Creek" was the place, and the 19th instant the time for an outbreak of this popular affection. The contracting parties, **Miss Beulah**, daughter of **Charles E. Carpenter, Esq.**, and **Mr. T. B. Jennings**, son of **George B. Jennings**, the **Rev. W. E. Gwatkin** the officiating clergyman. The ceremony was beautiful and impressive. The bride, handsomely attired in lavender silk, appeared the very embodiment of elegant grace and charming loveliness. The groom, clad in the neat, conventional black, "looked every inch the man." And bore himself splendidly. The occasion was an enjoyable one, the tables groaning under their sumptuous abundance, the guests manifesting a keen appreciation of the well ordered cuisine. On the following evening an old time reception was given at Church Hill, the residence of the groom's father, from seventy to eighty friends and kindred being invited to sample varied [illegible] adapted to the wants of the inner man, were the culinary appointments, after which the feast of reason and flow of soul, abated and, until the "cock crow" gave warning of approaching dawn.

06 Jul 1895 — **Elizabeth**, daughter of **Micajah Walker** (colored) was married on the 4th at Union Ridge Baptist church, to **Robert H. Baker** (colored) of Abingdon. The bride is a public school teacher of this county.

08 Jul 1895 — Licensed to marry by the Clerk of the County court: **Lewis M Bellamy** and **Annie M. Robinson**; **John P. Mann** and **Ida K. Rogers**.

09 Jul 1895 — Licensed to marry — county: **Leonard A. Chisholm** and **Virginia Fleming Scruggs**. The ceremony will take place in this city tomorrow. *[NOTE: This couple is on FindaGrave.com memorial pages #137425052 and #142392623.]*

10 Jul 1895 — The marriage of **Miss Nellie Toms** to **Mr. George Eubank** will take place this evening at the residence of **Mr. Wash Powell**, this county.

The marriage of **Miss Virginia Scruggs** of the Woolen Mills village to **Mr. Leonard Chisholm** of this city, took place at 4 o'clock this afternoon the parsonage of the Christian church, the pastor, the **Rev. W. A. Roush**, officiating.

11 Jul 1895 — A marriage license was issued in Washington Tuesday to **Charles L. Dawson** and **Sallie N. Dawson**, both of Nelson county.

17 Jul 1895 — The marriage of **Miss Virginia A. Burgess** to **Mr. Joseph F. Johnson**, both of the Woolen Mills village, took place at 3 o'clock this afternoon in this city.

18 Jul 1895 — Licensed to marry by the clerk of the County court: **James C. Pace** and **Miss Susan A. Barnett.**

A marriage license was issued in Washington yesterday to **Edward H. Webber** and **Leona G. Henry**, both of whom gave their residence as Charlottesville.

Sydney Putnam Owens, formerly of Richmond but now manager of the Norfolk branch of Dun's Mercantile Agency, and **Miss A. M. L'Ile** were married by **Dr. Hatch** at Grace Street Baptist church last evening, **Miss Lueh Thornhill** of Manchester was maid of honor, and **R. R. Owens, Jr.**, of Baltimore, the groom's brother, best man.

24 Jul 1895 — A PRETTY HOME WEDDING — A Daughter of Fluvanna Becomes a Happy Bride — At Lafayette Hill, Fluvanna county, the home of the bride occurred a pretty home wedding this morning at 10 o'clock. The contracting parties were **Mr. J. T. Omohundro** of Keswick and **Miss Maggie Wood** of Lafayette Hill.

The ceremony was performed by the **Rev. J. J. White** of Fluvanna and it was witnessed by a host of friends who warmly congratulated the happy pair.

25 Jul 1895 — TO GRETNA GREEN — "Love Laughs at Locksmiths" and Defies Stern Parents' Decrees — **Mr. J. W. Lane, Jr.**, and

Miss Mollie Shackelford hied away to Washington this morning on the 3:20 train upon matrimonial intentions bent.

The young lady is a daughter of **Mr. Z. N. Shackelford**, merchant, of this city and Mr. Lane is the son of **Mr. J. W. Lane**, principal of the Charlottesville public schools. It does not appear that any strenuous objection was raised to the young people joining their fortunes, but rather a fear of such led the groom, with the aid of his friend, **Mr. E. P. Wingfield**, to abstract the bride from her father's residence about eleven o'clock, when they proceeded to the house of a relative of the groom and awaited the coming of the train.

A telegram has been received by Mr. Wingfield from the groom saying, "Meet me on No. 1, everything O.K." *[NOTE: Findagrave.com memorials for this couple can be found at #127116542 and #127116535.]*

Ω葤

Division of the Slaves of Thomas Jackson, dec'd., Louisa County, VA February, 1802[4]

A division of the Slaves belonging to the Estate of Thomas Jackson D[ecease]d Agreeable to His Will among the Legatees.

Lot No.	Legatees	Enslaved People/ Value Assigned
1	Elizabeth Brittons children	Young Ben [£110]
2	William Jacksons children	James [£110]
3	Ann Christmas	Bartelett [£110]
4	Thomas Jackson	young Charles £100, Ben £15
5	Ann White	old Amy, Carroline & [D?]ooley £80, Hannah £36
6	Frances Anderson	Davey £90, Queen £25
7	Mary Parsons children	[Harry?] £90, Peter £15
8	John Jackson	Caty £65, young Amy £40
9	Charles Jackson	Old Charles £50, Phillis £12, Nick £75, Dick £15

Pursuant to a decree of Louisa Court bearing date the 8th day of February 1802 We the Subscribers have proceeded to value and allot the Slaves belonging to the Estate of Thomas Jackson decd. and upon ballotting for the same, so report that the different Legatees of Thomas Jackson decd. shall have the Slaves mentioned in the different Lots in the above Statement (viz.) Elizabeth Brittons children Lot No. 1, William Jacksons children Lot No. 2, Ann Christmas Lot. No.3, Thomas Jackson Lot No. 4, Ann White Lot No. 5, Frances Anderson Lot No. 6, Mary Parsons children Lot No. 7, John Jackson Lot No. 8, Charles Jackson Lot No. 9. Given under our hands this 16th day of February 1802

Thos Gardiner, Joel Walton [?], John Edwards, Saml. Overton

Ω葤

[4] Louisa County (Va.) Chancery Causes, 1753-1913. *Frances Anderson, Nelson Anderson, etc. vs. Exrs. Of Thomas Jackson etc., 1802-013.* Local Government Records Collection, Louisa County Court Records. The Library of Virginia, Richmond, Virginia. Selected and transcribed by Jean Cooper.

Shortwood Press, 2019 $12.00
ISBN: 978-1089782261

This book contains more than 2,500 names of testators whose wills appear in the Chancery Records Index for counties in Central Virginia, indexed by surname of the testator and the county where the testator resided.

Available at Amazon:
https://www.amazon.com/Hidden-Wills-Central-Virginia-Chancery/dp/1089782268

ผ ร ผ ร

2020 Officers of CVGA

Susan Lindsay, President
Linda Gore, Vice President
Pam Vandenhoff, Recording Secretary
Susan DuBar, Corresponding Secretary
Diane Inman, Treasurer & Membership Chair
Jean L. Cooper, Webmaster & Editor

Helpful Hint from Susan DuBar, CVGA Corresponding Secretary:

Don't be afraid to go back to FamilySearch.org for more information on people you've already researched on their site. They keep adding new material. (It's how I found out who my great-grandfather was.)

[Note: If you have a helpful hint for your fellow researchers, please email it to the editor at:
mailto:eleanordew@gmail.com *]*

ผ ร ผ ร

Good Will Hunting
by Anonymous

I search the courthouse records high and low
In hopes of finding that long lost will I know
Is in there somewhere waiting to be found.
All I need to do is run the thing to ground.
The ghost of the relative who left me his estate
Will be pleased that I claimed it even this late.
I know I'll find that missing document some way
And there will be a big payoff for me someday.

ผ ร ผ ร

Joel Parrish & Wife v. Executors of David Shepherd, et al.
Fluvanna County, Virginia, 1806-1808[5]

transcribed by Jean L. Cooper

[This Chancery case offers information on family relationships of the Parrish family of Fluvanna County. The transcriber has inserted corrections and comments in square brackets.]

[List of Plaintiffs and Defendants in the Complaint of Joel Parrish & Wife v. Executors of David Shepherd, et al. as of January 25th 1808]

- Joel Parrish and Nancy, his wife
- Martin Baskett and Frances, his wife
- Randolph Perry and Polly, his wife
- John Shepherd
- Samuel Cocke, administrator of the estate of his late wife Elizabeth deceased,
- James Barnett and Joanna, his wife, and
- William Kent, administrator of the estate of his late wife Annis deceased,
  [Note: "Nancy, Frances, Polly, John, Elizabeth, Joanna, and Annis were children of John Shepherd, deceased"]
  against
- David Shepherd and Christopher Shepherd, executors of the last will and testament of John Shepherd decd. (defendants)

☙

Bill of Complaint

To the Court of Fluvanna County in Chancery sitting Your orators and oratrixes Joel Parrish and Nancy his wife, Martin Basket and

Frances his wife, Randolph Perry & Polly his wife, John Shepherd, Samuel Cocke administrator to his decd. wife Elizabeth Cocke, James Bernard and Joanna his wife & William Kent administrator to his decd. wife Annis Kent decd. who said Nancy, Frances, Polly, John, Elizabeth, Joanna, and Annis were children & legatees of John Shepherd decd. humbly complaining show to the Court that on or about the ____ day of _____ 17__ the sd. Jno. Shepherd departed this life first having made and executed his last will and testament whereby he lent to his beloved wife Mary during her natural life the plantation & land whereon he then lived, with all her stock of horses, cows, hogs and sheep, household and kitchen furniture, plantation and blacksmith tools and all his negroes except two specifically bequeathed to his daughters Joanna and Annis. That by the said will the testator bequeathed to your orator John forty one pounds eighteen shillings more than an equal part [will?] the rest of his sons, to your oratrixes Mary, Joanna & Nancy he bequeathed fifty pounds each, to Elizabeth Cocke the decd. wife and intestatrix of your orator Samuel he bequeathed fifty pounds and to Annis the decd. wife and intestatrix of your orator William he bequeathed fifty pounds to be raised out of his estate after the death of his wife. And after sundry other clauses the sd. Testator directs that if after all his just debts (and the legacies aforesaid) are paid, these should be any remainder either by bill bond or otherwise the same shall be equally divided amongst all his children or their legal representatives. And finally appoints David and Christopher Shepherd executors to sd. will who took upon themselves the execution of the same. Your orators and oratrixes further shew that

---

[5] Fluvanna County (Va.) Chancery Causes, 1779-1882. *Joel Parrish & Wife v. Executors of David Shepherd, etc, 1808-003*. Local Government Records Collection, Fluvanna County Court Records. The Library of Virginia, Richmond, Virginia.

although the sd. Mary is not dead, yet that she has voluntarily relinquished to the sd. executors (defendants hereto) the whole estate lent to her as aforesd. except two negroes by the name of Sam & Jack, one grey horse & saddle, a feather bed and furniture, a cow & calf with provisions for one year the still and wheat fan with a few other trifling articles as will more fully appear by reference to an instrument of writing under the hand and seal of sd. Mary which is hereunto annexed, that by said relinquishment the part of sd. estate so contained in the well in the same manner as if the sd. Mary had departed this life. Your orators & oratrixes further state that the estate relinquished as aforesd. Consists of, a tract of land, several slaves, to wit, stock, and a variety of other personal property – all of what except the land your orators & oratrixes are informed and believe has been taken possession of & sold by the executors except the negroes, & some beds, and for [the?] that it is impossible to make an equal division of the slaves aforesd. After satisfying the specific legacies aforesd. without a sale of the negroes and any other property relinquished to the executors as aforesd. which may remain unsold. And out of the proceeds of the sales already made as aforesd. And the proceeds of the sales to be made that the executors be decreed first to pay and satisfy the specific legacies to your orator John, your oratrixes Mary, Joann and Nancy and their husbands, and to the sd. Samuel Cocke and William Kent the specific Legacies to their decd. wives respectively. And to divide the residue if any equally amongst Your orators & oratrixes and themselves as the legal representatives [aforesd.] Jno. Shepherd decd. your orators & oratrixes pray the C[ommon]wealth's [illegible] [Bill of Complaint stops here.]

ॐ

Statement of Mary Shepherd
(23 November 1807)

Know all men by these presents that I, Mary Shepherd, widow and Relict of John Shepherd Dec'd being in the possession of the greater part of sd. John Shepherd's Estate which was by sd. descendants last Will & Testament sent to me during natural life. But finding my Plantation affairs in a Ruinous Condition and Age and Infirmities fast Advancing on me, have on these Considerations thought proper an deem it Prudent to Relinquish my Right and Title in sd. Estate except a Small part for my Support during the Short time I expect to want a Subsistence. That is to say I do Reserve to myself Two Negroes by the name of Sam & Jack, one Grey Horse & my saddle a Feather Bed & furniture a Cow & Calf with provisions for one year the Mill & Wheat [illegible] with a few Other Trifleing Articles –

All the Residue of sd. Estate both Real and Personal I have and do by these presents Relinquish to my two sons David & Christopher Shepherd executors to the last Will & Testament of my Husband desiring them to dispose of the same as if my decease had Actually taken taken place. In Witness whereof I have hereunto set my hand and Seal this 23 day of November 1807.

N.B. The words last Will & Testament and of sd. Estate Interlined before assigned.

Mary (her Mark: X) Shepherd
Henry A. Bryant
Augustine Shepherd

ॐ

Proceeds from Sale of Slaves and Sundry Other Property of John Shepherd, Deceased (24 October 1808)

In obedience to an order and Decree from the worshipful Court of Fluvanna County we whose names are hereunto Subscribed Commissioners named in sd. Order and decree, Attended in person at the Sale on the premises of John Shepherd dec'd. On the 27thday of Jany. 1808 which sale had been lawfully Advertised previous thereto at which time the Slaves and Sundry Other property was exposed to public Sale to the highest bidder on a credit of Twelve Months and was Sold as follows, To Wit

Purchaser	Name of enslaved person	value in pounds
David Shepherd	Rachel & Major, her child	117.5.0
Martin Baskett	(little) Charles	49.10.0
Joel Parrish jr.	Beck	80.0.0
Martin Baskett	Winston	90.6.0
James Barnett	James	75.0.0
James Kent	Stephen	125.0.0
David Shepherd	Charles	135.0.0
		672.1.0

Sundry Other Articles of property Sold at the first Sale together with property sold this day Amounting in all to 180.1.7.[6]

---

[6] This shorthand format represents pounds (£), shillings (s), and pence (d), and would be written £180.1s.7d. The American "colonists used several overlapping currencies, all linked to the English monetary system." (Walbert) But why did the British system continue to be used in the new American states, as late as 1820? For more information on money in the colonies and early republic, see Walbert, David, "The Value of Money in Colonial America." in *NCpedia.org*.
https://www.ncpedia.org/anchor/value-money-colonial-america ; and Michener, Rob, "Money in the American

Bonds with Securities taken by the Executors and the proceeds to be Applied agreeable to the order hereunto An[n]exed Given under Our hands this 24th day of October 1808.

Jonathan Stanley
John Bryant
Hutchins Barnett

ೞ ഌ ೞ ഌ

List of Amelia County (VA) Sheriffs, 1735-2021[7]

Amelia County was created in 1735 from parts of Prince George and Brunswick counties. Parts of the county were later carved out to create Prince Edward and Nottoway counties.

Sheriff	Term Began	Term Ended
John Burton	Unknown	1735
Charles Irby	1735	1739
Thomas Tabb	1739	1741
Abraham Green	1741	1743
Samuel Tarry	1743	1745
George Walker	1745	1747
William Watson	1747	1749
Abraham Cock	1749	1751
Richard Booker	1751	1753
William Clement	1753	1755
Samuel Tarry	1755	1757
William Archer	1757	1759
Wood Jones	1759	1761
Henry Ward	1761	1763
David Greenhill	1763	1765
Richard Jones	1765	1768
William Crawley	1770	1771
John Booker, Jr.	1771	1776
Benjamin Ward	1776	1777

Colonies." In EH.net (Economic History Association), https://eh.net/encyclopedia/money-in-the-american-colonies/
[7] "Sheriff History" on the website of the Virginia Sheriffs' Association, https://vasheriff.org/sheriffs-resources/sheriff-history [Note: Information on Sheriff History page provided by Sheriffs' Offices, Sheriffs' Offices' websites, and the Virginia Sheriffs' Association.]

John Royall	1777	1778
Vivian Brooking	1778	1780
Lawrence Wells	1780	1782
Christopher Hudson	1782	1786
Christopher Ford	1786	1787
Francis Gooch	1787	1788
Stephen Cocke	1788	1789
Edmund Booker	1789	1790
Edmund Booker, Jr.	1790	1792
John Booker	1792	1794
John Ogilby	1794	1795
Davis Booker	1795	1797
John Archer	1797	1800
Joshua Chaffin	1800	1802
Thomas T. Wills	1802	1811
Samuel Ford	1811	1814
D. Edward Eggleston	1814	1816
Joshua Chaffin, Jr.	1816	1818
James P. Cocke	1818	1819
Rodophil Jeter	1819	1821
Tilmond E. Jeter	1821	1824
Richard Eggleston	1824	1827
Henry H. Southall	1827	1829
Dabney Miller	1829	1830
John Webster	1830	1832
John P. Bolling	1832	1834
Thomas W. Webster	1834	1837
Henry P. Eanes	1837	1840
Hodijah Meade	1840	1841
Austin Seay	1841	1842
Edward Green	1842	1844
James P. Cocke	1844	1845
Henry H. Southall	1845	1848
David Maben	1848	1849
Matthew Allen	1849	1851
John A. Jeter	1851	1852
William P. Jeter	1852	1856
Aaron Haskins	1856	1865
John H. Haskins	1865	1866
Chamberline Coleman	1866	1870
John W. Leidig	1870	1871
S.B.R. Loving	1870	1870
Thomas S. Scott	1871	1873
A.C. Tucker	1873	1881
W.T. Vaughan	1881	1887
W.E. Coleman	1887	1899
W.J. Elam	1899	1912
A.H. Perdue	1912	1951
John F. Duke	1951	1960
Harold Osborne	1975	1988

Jimmy E. Weaver	1988	2008
Ricky L. Walker	2008	Present

◓ ◔ ◓ ◔

List of Greene County (VA) Sheriffs, 1838-2021

Greene County was established in 1838 from Orange County. The information in this table is courtesy of Greene County Sheriff Steven S. Smith. Research on the pre-Civil War sheriffs was done by Joe Freni in 2012.

Sheriff	Term Began	Term Ended
William Parrott[8]	1838	1840
Thomas Davis	1840	1842
James Simms	1842	1843
Daniel White	1844	1845
Oliver Fink	1845	1847
James Fink	1848	1849
David Miller	Jan. 1849	Mar. 1851
D. Blakey	Feb. 1852	1859
Benjamin F. Robinson	1860	1868
Joseph Smith	1869	1903
William App Crawford	1904	1907
Russell Melone	1908	Mar. 1937
W. T. ("Willie") Snow	Mar. 1937	1943
Russell Melone	1944	Aug. 1947
George Ed Morris	Aug. 1947	Nov. 1949
William D. ("Hooks") Deane	Nov. 1949	1971
Harold Chapman	1972	1983
William L. Morris	1984	2003
J. S. ("Scott") Haas	2004	2011
Steven S. Smith	2012	present

---

[8] William Parrott was the first Greene County sheriff. He was appointed to the post at the age of 84.

List of Appomattox County (VA) Sheriffs, 1845-2021[9]

Appomattox County was formed in 1845 from Buckingham, Prince Edward, Campbell and Charlotte counties. In 1848, another part from Campbell County was added. This list of sheriffs is not complete, but we will continue to research. This list is used courtesy of the Virginia Sheriffs' Association.

Sheriff	Term Began	Term Ended
S. P. Coleman	Unknown	Unknown
T. B. Bryant	Unknown	Unknown
Willis Arthur Plunkett	Unknown	Unknown
William H. Gills	Unknown	Unknown
W. T. Johnson	Unknown	Unknown
William Parris	Unknown	Unknown
George T. Peers	Unknown	Unknown
Joel Watkins	1845	Unknown
Frank W. McKinney	1903	1916
H. W. McKinney	1940	Unknown
David T. Robertson	1960	1960
Walter Conner	1960	1963
L. L. Stanley	1963	1971
J. E. Richardson	1971	1996
O. Wilson Staples	1996	2012
Barry E. Letterman	2012	2019
Donald D. Simpson	2020	present

---

[9] "Sheriff History" on the website of the Virginia Sheriffs' Association, https://vasheriff.org/sheriffs-resources/sheriff-history [Note: Information on Sheriff History page provided by Sheriffs' Offices, Sheriffs' Offices' websites, and the Virginia Sheriffs' Association.]

FIFTEEN DOLLARS REWARD

From the *Richmond Enquirer*, 18 Feb 1806.

Ran-away from the Washington Tavern, on the 25th Dec. last, a Mulatto Man by the name of LEWIS, about 25 years of age. This fellow was formerly the property of Edward Garland of Hanover, was sold to Mr. Shields of Goochland, and while the property of the said Shields, travelled very considerably doubt but he will attempt to pass for a free man, to the contrary of which may be discovered by attending to his person: he is about 5 feet 9 or 10 inches high, with rather an intelligent countenance when spoken to, and is a very well made fellow; indeed he has not a bushy head for a fellow of his colour, being tolerably light; nor has he any marks by which he may be particularly known, other than those already mentioned, and that of his extreme politeness. He has a wife living in the estate of Mr. Watkins of Goochland, at a place called Dover Mills; yet his very general acquaintance may subject him to be caught elsewhere, perhaps in Lexington, in the county of Rockbridge (Virginia) at which place he lived for some time prior to his being my property. He is a very good barber, and perhaps may attempt that calling for a support in some of the remote towns of Virginia. Nevertheless if he is secured in any jail within the state of Virginia so that I can get him again, or delivered to me in the City of Richmond, I will give the above reward and reasonable charges.

EDWARD HALLAM

February 4 [1806]

ଔ ଵ ଔ ଵ

Cary Family (Virginia and Maryland)[10]

by Jean L. Cooper

Wilson Miles Cary (2 Sep 1806-9 Jan 1877) was the son of Wilson Jefferson Cary (1783-1823) of Fluvanna County, Virginia, and his wife, Virginia Randolph (1786-1852). Mrs. Cary was the sister of Thomas Mann Randolph, Jr., a son-in-law of President Thomas Jefferson. Wilson Miles Cary first attended Hampden-Sydney College, then the University of Virginia in session 1, enrolling on March 9, 1825, and being expelled October 6, 1825. (UVA Matriculation books)

Wilson was among a group of students expelled for conducting a "a serious riot and disturbance" on Oct. 1, 1825. The faculty met on Oct. 2 and 3 about this matter, and then handed the issue to the Board of Visitors to determine the punishment for those involved. The faculty minutes summarized Cary's statement:

Wilson Miles Carey was not intoxicated; made no noise; was laid hold of by Mr. [George] Tucker but escaped and afterwards by Dr. Emmet, who tore a counterpane which witness had around him as well as his shirt sleeve; was seized by two Professors but not at the same time; heard the language regarding the European Professors; did not use it himself; thinks he did aim a blow at Professor Emmet; cried a rescue; said in allusion to Professor E, "the damn'd rascal has torn my shirt"; conceived he was assaulted and therefore acted as he did; had no intention when he left his Dormitory to make any disturbance; took up a brick expecting that Dr. Emmet would stand back and be intimidated; was not of the party who took up sticks; did not throw any brick or stick; does not recollect having been asked his name by Dr. Emmet. (UVa Faculty Minutes, Oct. 2-5, 1825)

The Board of Visitors determined that Cary should be expelled:

A communication from the Faculty of Professors is rec[ei]ved in the following words, to wit, "University of Virginia. Ordered that Wilson Miles Carey having on the night of the 1st. instant resisted the authority of a Professor, used

---

[10] Originally published April 7, 2020, in the blog *Students of the University of Virginia, 1825-1874*. https://uvastudents.wordpress.com/2020/04/07/two-members-of-the-cary-family-virginia/

violence against him, and excited others to follow his example, and for abusive epithets concerning the said Professor, be expelled from the University." Copied from the minutes of the Faculty. Robley Dunglison Secretary. George Tucker. (*UVa Board of Visitors Minutes*, Oct. 6, 1825)

Subsequently, Cary studied law with Judge Brockenbrough and Judge Henry St. George Tucker, and was admitted to the bar in Charlottesville, Virginia.[11] He married Jane Margaret Carr (1809-1903) in 1831. Their children were Sarah Nicholas, Virginia (died in infancy), Hetty, Virginia Randolph, Wilson-Miles Jr., John Brune, Jane Margaret, and Sydney Carr Cary. (*The Virginia Carys*) Hetty Cary was a famous Southern belle and Confederate spy. Her sister Jane ("Jenny") set the words of the poem "Maryland, My Maryland" to a tune called "Lauriger Horatius." The combination later became the Maryland State Song.)

After his marriage, Cary practiced law in Charlottesville and was the editor of the Virginia Advocate newspaper. He also served in the local militia and was called "Colonel" Cary all his life.

In 1833, Wilson Miles Cary and his family moved to Baltimore, Maryland, where Cary practiced law for a time. In 1835, he bought a farm in Baltimore County called "Haystack," and "was engaged in agricultural pursuits" for some years. (*Baltimore Sun* Jan. 10, 1877)

Cary was elected to the Maryland Senate, and served in that body from 1846-1852.

The Carys established a school for young ladies at Haystack. In 1850, the family moved into Baltimore. The school was continued in Baltimore as the Southern Home School and was in existence at least through 1906, when it was listed as a girls' preparatory school in *Patterson's American Education*.

Wilson Miles Cary senior died in 1877, in Baltimore County, Maryland, and is buried in Saint Thomas Episcopal Church Cemetery, in Owings Mills, Maryland. (FindaGrave.com)

His son, Wilson-Miles Cary, Jr. (12 Dec. 1838-28 Aug. 1914), was born at "Haystack" in Baltimore County, Maryland. He attended the University of Virginia in sessions 33-34 (1856-1858). He served in the Confederate army as a captain and major in the Quartermaster Department. After the Civil War, he established a classical boys' school in Baltimore, and then became a lawyer and served as the Clerk of the Criminal Court of Baltimore. He later became a genealogist, and had articles published in various genealogical and historical periodicals, as well as writing a novel, *Sally Cary; a long hidden romance of Washington's life*. Cary Jr. never married and had no children. (Death certificate)

He is buried at Saint Thomas Episcopal Church Cemetery in Owings Mills, Maryland, with his mother and father.

References:
- Cary, Wilson-Miles (1838-1914), Virginia Death Certificate #18560.

---

[11] Law students were allowed to study (or "read") law with individual attorneys and judges, in order to take the bar examination. In fact, Virginia is still one of only four states that allow one to take the bar exam without going to law school. https://barexam.virginia.gov/reader/readerrules.html

- "Death of Wilson M. Cary." *Baltimore Sun*, Jan. 10, 1877, p.1.
- Wilson Miles Cary tombstone. Findagrave.com.
- Durham, Stephanie; Kibler, Neelie; and Noble, Natalie. "Wilson Miles Cary." *Mr. Jefferson's Academical Village: The Early History of the University* [website] https://pages.shanti.virginia.edu/Early_Life_at_UVA/wilson-miles-cary/ (Note: The son—Wilson Miles Cary—attributed to Wilson-Miles Cary Jr. in the Noble article was the son of his brother, John Brune Cary.)
- Harrison, Fairfax. *The Virginia Carys: An Essay in Genealogy*. New York, 1919, p.115-117.
- *Jefferson's University… the early life.* [website] http://juel.iath.virginia.edu/home
- *Patterson's American Education*. 1906. Vol. 3, p. 284.
- *University of Virginia. Faculty Minutes*, 1st session, 1825. http://juel.iath.virginia.edu/exist/cocoon/juel/juel_one?doc=/db/JUEL/faculty/Sessions/session-001.xml&key=P26928#m1
- *University of Virginia. Board of Visitor's Minutes*. Oct. 3-6, 1825. http://juel.iath.virginia.edu/exist/cocoon/juel/juel_one?doc=/db/JUEL/BOV/1820/bov_18251003.xml&key=P26928#m1
- *University of Virginia Matriculation Books, 1825-1904*, Accession #RG-14/4/2.041, Special Collections Dept., University of Virginia Library, Charlottesville, Va.

Charles William Cary
(20 Sep 1826-23 Aug 1852)[12]
by Jean L. Cooper

Charles William Cary was the son of Captain Cyrus Cary (1794-1832) of Lewisburg, Greenbrier County, Virginia (now West Virginia), and his wife Mary Skiles Arbuckle. (FindaGrave.com) Cyrus Cary was a member of the Virginia Legislature from Greenbrier County in the session of 1829-1830.

Charles first attended the Virginia Military Institute, graduating in 1848. He then attended the University of Virginia in sessions 25-26 (1848-1850), where he studied medicine. In 1851, he graduated from the Medical College of Philadelphia. (*VMI Historical Rosters Database, UVA Matriculation Books*, Gayley)

Dr. Cary apparently started his practice in Lewisburg but died there in 1852 of consumption at "Montescena," the home of his Uncle David S. Creigh. (NRHP Form) Though there is no grave marker, Dr. Cary was buried at Old Stone Presbyterian Church in Lewisburg.

References:
- Cary, Charles William. Findagrave.com https://www.findagrave.com/memorial/105708127/charles-william-cary
- "Charles William Cary" (Roster ID 89) in the *Virginia Military Institute Historical Rosters Database*. https://archivesweb.vmi.edu/rosters/record.php?ID=89

---

[12] Originally published April 8, 2020, in the blog *Students of the University of Virginia, 1825-1874*. https://uvastudents.wordpress.com/2020/04/08/charles-william-cary-20-sep-1826-23-aug-1852/

- Harrison, Fairfax. *The Virginia Carys: An Essay In Genealogy*. New York, 1919, p.147-148.
- Gayley, James F. *A history of the Jefferson Medical College of Philadelphia*. Philadelphia, 1858, p. 50.
- National Register of Historic Places Registration Form: Montescena. http://www.wvculture.org/shpo/nr/pdf/greenbrier/75001888.pdf
- Turk, Mrs. Rudolph Samuel. *Beatty-Asfordby; the ancestry of John Beatty and Susanna Asfordby with some of their descendants*. Frank Allaben Genealogical Company, 1909. Generations 3 and 4.
- *University of Virginia Matriculation Books, 1825-1904*, Accession #RG-14/4/2.041, Special Collections Dept., University of Virginia Library, Charlottesville, Va.

ભ ᖫ ભ ᖫ

Estate of Elias Palmer, dec'd., Campbell County, VA, 1833-34[13]

transcribed by Jean L. Cooper

Bill of Complaint

To the worshipful the County Court of Campbell in Chancery sit[t]ing humbly complaining sheweth to your Worships your Orators & Oratrixes, Clarke Hubbard & Lucy his wife formerly Lucy Palmer, Elizabeth Fourgurian & Hannah Palmer; which said Lucy, Elizabeth & Hannah were children of Elias Palmer dec'd. Elias P. Light, John Light, Stephen Light & Joel Light (the said Joel being

hereafter made Deft.) were children of Mary Light who was also a daughter of the sd. Decedent. Your complainants represent and state that Elias Palmer on the 11th of September 1822 made and published his last will & testament and that on the 27th September 1827 he made & published a codicil to the sd. [said] Will, and by the sd. Will he appointed Reuben D. Palmer & John [T?] Palmer his Exr. and afterwards on the ___ day of September 1833 departed this life.

Your complainants present, that at a monthly term holden in and for the County of Halifax the sd. Reuben D. Palmer one of the Exr proved said will qualified as the Exc. & gave bond & security according to law & is now the sole acting Executor. Your complainants state that their testator among other things directed that his personal estate should be divided between his children by name to wit Lucy Hubbard, Elizabeth Fourgurian, Reuben D. Palmer, Hannah Palmer & Susan Fuqua one sixth part to each of them to all the remaining part of his estate not before disposed of after his just debts are paid & the remaining sixth to be equally divided between the children of Mary Light.

Your complainants further state that there is in the hands of the Executor funds sufficient to Pay off all the debts & legacies without resorting to a sale of the slaves, and that it is the wish and desire of all the parties to have a division of the slaves belonging to said estate; but that cannot be done without the aid of this worshipful court because Joel Light one of the persons interested in the said division is a minor under the age of twenty one years.
To the end therefore that speedy justice be done all parties and a division decreed your

[13] Campbell County (Va.) Chancery Causes, 1794-1946. *Clark Hubbard & Wife, etc., vs. Exr. of Elias Palmer, etc. Index no. 1834-008.* Local Government Records Collection, Campbell County Court Records. The Library of Virginia, Richmond, Virginia.

complainants pray that Reuben D. Palmer, Joel Light & Henry A. Christian & Susan B. his wife formerly Susan Palmer, be made party defendants to this their bill, and that the Court make such further orders & decree as shall seem proper by this worshipfull Court and in duty bound they will [illegible] pray etc. etc.

[Notes on back of bill]: Persons named as commissioners: Wm. Coats, Elisha Barksdale, Daniel Palmer, Wm Hurt, Edward T. White, Wm. C. Coats, Wm P. Barksdale or any three of them.]

ℬ

Division of Slaves of Estate of Elias Palmer, dec'd.

In obedience to a Decree of the County Court of Campbell made at the December Term 1833 [illegible] The undersigned commissioners divided the Slaves belonging to the Est. of Elias Palmer dec'd. in the following manner, to wit—

To Elizabeth Fourgurian Lot no. 1, consisting of
       Mount [Sumer?] $600.00
       Coleman $300.00
       Liddy $30.00
       Mary $50.00
[Total] $980.00
To receive from lot.3 6.33 1/3
[Total] $986.33 1/3

Lot no. 2 to Hannah Palmer
Washington $600.00
       Ben 200.00
       Ellen 163.00
[Total] $963.00
To receive from Lot No.3 $7.33 1/3
To receive from Lot No.5 $13.00
To receive from Lot No.6 $3.00

[Total] $986.33 1/3

Lot no. 3 To Lucy Hubbard
       Jacob $500.00
       Billy $500.00
[Total] $1000.00
To pay lot no.1 $6.33 1/3
To pay lot no.2 $7.33 1.3
[SubTotal] 13.66 2/3
[Total] $986.33 1/3

Lot No. 4 To Reuben D. Palmer
       Anthony $600.00
       Rheba & Child 300.00
       Rosa 75.00
[Total] 975.00
To receive from Lot No.5 $.66 2/3
To receive from Lot no.6 $10.66 2/3
[Subtotal] 11.33 1/3
[Total] $986.33 1/3

Lot No. 5 To Elias P. Light, Jno. Light, Stephen Light, & Joel Light
       Daniel $600.00
       Parthena $400.00
[Total] $1000.00
To Pay lot no.4 $ .66 2/3
To Pay lot no.2 $13.00
[Subtotal] 13.66 2/3
[Total] $986.33 1/3

Lot No. 6 To H. B. Christian
       Ned $425.00
       John $150.00
       Peyton $425.00
[Total] $1000.00
To pay lot no.3 $3.00
To pay not. No.4 $10.66 2/3
[Subtotal] 13.66 2/3
[Total] $986.33 1/3